# The Alexander Technique

a personal perspective

## Seeing with Fresh Eyes

Gentian Rahtz

The Alexander Technique: Seeing with Fresh Eyes. A Personal Perspective.

Copyright © Gentian Rahtz 2022.

Gentian Rahtz has asserted her right to be identified as the author of this work, in accordance with the Copyright, Design and Patents Act, 1988.

Cover: Don Burton (1943–1996), Director of Fellside School 1986–1996. Design by Dawn Collins.

ISBN 978-1-3999-1406-2

*for my grandchildren*
*Oscar and Jasper*

# Contents

# Acknowledgements

I would like to express appreciation and gratitude to my editor and proofreader Paul Parkyn for his thorough and patient efforts on my behalf.

Both he and Jill Rahtz have offered perceptive comments, although the content was relatively unfamiliar to them both. I have had constructive feedback from several Alexander teachers, including Judy Hammond, Lucia Walker and Jean Fischer. It was Sheila Hamnett who said that the chapters she had read had re-awakened her interest in Alexander, which subsequently influenced my approach to this book. I am also indebted to Rufus Wondre, Jay Aspen and my page setter Erin McGowan for their technological expertise.

Miranda Tufnell, who has both an Alexander and creative arts background, has given me invaluable help with clarifying the structure, content and rationale of this book.

# Introduction

The title, 'Seeing with Fresh Eyes', reflects the Alexander Technique's emphasis on rediscovering our birthright, 'the natural good use of ourselves', that most of us had as young children, which includes seeing the world afresh. Pieces of creative writing extend the frame of reference for the Technique, and for its close connections with the natural environment.

While there may be growing support for a more holistic and embodied approach to Alexander teaching, such as the Contemporary Alexander School in the United States, the fact remains that many people find that Pilates and yoga, mindfulness, and other body/mind techniques are more accessible and easier to understand.

This book offers an overview, a personal perspective, written to stimulate new interest in the unique character of the Technique and bring it more to life. It should appeal to people who are intrigued by the subtle relationship of mind and muscle, and may inspire those who are thinking of exploring this practice, or even training as an Alexander teacher.

The Alexander Community may be interested in chapters with a more contemporary character such as *The Alchemy of the Alexander Technique, Our Bipedal Inheritance* and *Body*

*Memory*. The chapters on *Coming to our Senses* and *Coming to Rest* highlight the importance of our kinaesthetic sense, which facilitates a more embodied awareness of how the classic thought processes of the Technique influence our sense of ourselves.

One of the hallmarks of this practice is quiet, skilled hands-on work with a teacher, which reflects people back to themselves. They learn to be more aware of the quality of their attention, of how they move and relate to their surroundings. This process clarifies their capacity for personal change, for finding an inner compass. They may say that they feel witnessed at a deep level, akin to some forms of counselling.

The phrase 'The Alexander Technique' remains the most familiar term but is now often referred to as 'Alexander', after the name of its founder, as is Pilates. Many of F M Alexander's phrases were of his time, so some have been updated to bring them more in line with present-day usage.

*** 

This book must start with a weekend in 1985 that changed my life. I was curious about the Alexander Technique, so I went on an introductory weekend run by Don Burton in the Lake District, where he was starting a new school in Kendal, Fellside Alexander School.

I remember going to a café at lunchtime during this weekend after some hands-on work with Don — it was perfect May weather — and being unable to speak. I was aware of feeling an inner stillness and silence. The experience of how my body felt, how I felt about myself, was so novel, so surprising, I was taken aback, indeed quite literally into my back, which felt newly alive and part of myself — I had a sense of the vitality of my spine, of having a back as well as a front!

This was my first experience of the power of Alexander touch. It did not feel imposed upon me — almost the opposite — as if Don had made himself porous, or transparent, so little did he try to correct me in any way. His hands 'listened' to my system in a way that awakened some awareness of an innate intelligence in the tissues of my body that had not been heard in that way before.

I subsequently joined the three-year Alexander teacher training course at Fellside Alexander School in 1986 and have enjoyed teaching the Technique in a variety of settings for thirty years.

\*\*\*

References to Don Burton's teaching have been included in several sections. His valuable insights and in-depth approach have been a formative influence on many students, including myself. Don's very finely judged hands-on work, his master classes in anatomy, physiology and embryology and his understanding of the complexities of body and psyche were impressive. His teaching embodied his belief that his students' holistic personal development was a crucial part of their training as teachers, and he saw the need to balance the training of their  thought processes with kinaesthetic awareness. His death in 1996 has been a great loss to the profession.

# Chapter 1
## Historical Aspects

## F M Alexander's Biography

Frederick Matthias Alexander (1869-1955) was born in Tasmania. He grew up in an evangelical Protestant household, the eldest of eight children alive at adulthood and was home-educated on a large isolated farm, which probably nurtured his independence of spirit. He must have enjoyed the freedom of movement as he rode his horse in the surrounding wide-open spaces and this may have influenced his later discoveries.

From an early age, he had a passion for horses, rode all his life and enjoyed horse racing. His mother, a midwife in the remote outback, would jump on her horse to attend a birth. Alexander doubtless honed his observational skills while watching how horses moved with such grace and co-ordination. On several occasions, a win at the races rescued him and his family from recurring debt.

He learnt to play the violin and was keenly interested in the theatre, with a life-long love of Shakespeare. He moved to Melbourne when he was twenty, and later to Sydney, to find work as a declamatory actor, although his father called him a 'strolling player and a vagabond.' His parents were both the offspring of convicts and Alexander himself was always evasive about his convict ancestry. He distanced himself from his father, and throughout his life was conscious of his relative lack of formal education and humble origins.

Alexander's birth was premature, which gave him breathing problems at birth and during his childhood. It was not long before he began to have problems with losing his voice whilst performing. Doctors advised him to rest his voice, but the problem still returned once he was back on stage. It is significant that the doctors only examined his throat. Threatened with surgery by his now flummoxed doctors, he made the crucial deduction that underpins his Technique — that *something he was doing whilst on stage was undermining his voice.* This precipitated years of patient self-observation, including many hours in front of mirrors, when he came to notice how the use of his whole body was affecting his throat and his voice. He realised that how he stood and moved whilst reciting increased postural tension throughout his spine, which affected the hang of his larynx and thus strained his voice, a habit that was not so present in his everyday life.

Alexander had discovered that *how* we habitually move or use our bodies in everyday life critically affects function throughout the whole body. It then took many years of trial and experiment for Alexander to understand how to overcome his postural habits. As he so aptly said, '*change involves carrying out an activity against the habits of a life-time.*'

One of the most remarkable aspects of Alexander's long and patient process of discovery was that there were no precursors — he was not building on the earlier exploratory work of other people.

A big win on the horses made it possible for Alexander to move to London in 1904 and to a country seen as 'home' to many people who grew up in the outposts of the British empire; he also knew that London had famous theatres. Initially, he arrived there with letters of recommendation from several Australian doctors, but he also promoted himself in a series of pamphlets to explain his discoveries as 'founder of a respiratory method' along with the 'cultivation and development of the human voice'. As he later said, 'in those days you couldn't get on here [in London] unless you appeared to be the right sort,' so he accordingly acquired a manservant, a smart address and a fine wardrobe; he apparently charged four guineas an hour, a large fee at the time.

In London, he continued to teach his ideas to actors, musicians, vocalists and dancers and gained valuable support from the medical community who gave him other referrals. During both world wars, he built a thriving practice in the United States.

He had substantial success with his work but in later life became rather embittered by the refusal of Western medicine and education to recognise the importance of his ideas. He had influential and loyal supporters in both London and America, including Aldous Huxley. John Dewey, after many sessions with Alexander, said that he considered that the Technique should be at the heart of all systems of education, because it was about 'learning how to learn.'

Alexander wrote four books: *Man's Supreme Inheritance* (1910), *Constructive Conscious Control of the Individual* (1924), *The Use of the Self* (1932), and *The Universal Constant in Living* (1942), which contain details of the development of his discoveries.

In London, he eventually started a training school for teachers in 1930 and some of these students later set up Alexander schools themselves, where they developed their own individual styles of teaching. Two of these teachers, Walter and Dilys Carrington, took over the school started by Alexander.

This was also the school where my teacher, Don Burton, qualified in 1973. Don subsequently became director of Fellside Alexander School in Kendal, Cumbria in 1986, from where I qualified as an Alexander teacher in 1990.

Fellside was a very innovative and influential training school with a large number of students and many visiting teachers. Accordingly, my lineage from Alexander himself is that of a third-generation teacher.

**Michael Bloch** has written a fascinating biography: *The Life of F M Alexander*. 2004.

# Historical Influences on
# F M Alexander's Discoveries

It feels significant that F M Alexander (1869–1955) made his discoveries in the first half of the 20th century, at a time of fundamental and wide ranging changes in his world. We, also, are in the throes of major cultural, social, scientific, environmental and technological change, which will inevitably colour our perception of his original contributions.

He was alive at a time when there was an intense struggle for control between scientific and religious thought. Charles Darwin's profoundly influential book, 'On the Origin of the Species by Means of Natural Selection', had been published in 1859 — ten years before Alexander's birth.

He lived through two world wars and the Great Depression of the early 1930's. Women were still wearing corsets and he would have been aware of the fight for women's suffrage movement (the right to vote).

There were many strands of historical thought that fed the assumption that the mind was superior, more elevated than the body, and that thoughtful reasoning could solve many social problems. The 19th century was also marked by great optimism about science. Influences from the 17th and 18th centuries, 'the age of reason,' emphasised rational, scientific, objective observation, including evidence from the senses, but probably not including subjective bodily feedback, such as that from the kinaesthetic sense.

The West adopted the Greek Platonic and then later the Christian concept of prioritising the soul and the spirit over the flesh. In addition, the Greek philosophers had identified reason, a uniquely human faculty, as the link to divinity, which meant that other living creatures, lacking reason, missed out on divinity. This distinction between humans and the rest of the natural world went on to become a central theme in Victorian thought, with disastrous long-term consequences for the natural world. As mind and matter were seen as separate, so were man and nature.

These ideas have had a profound effect on philosophical, intellectual, and cultural thinking in Western Europe for more than 2000 years and still influence our educational and health systems. The concept of subtle energy flow or 'qi' in the body, which is taken for granted in much of Eastern medicine, is still not accepted by Western medicine.

It is worth noting that the East, with its Daoist and Buddhist cultural influences, had historically developed a more nuanced approach to understanding the relationship between mind and body, although there were, inevitably, a range of disparate influences in both East and West in this respect.

Those ideas prevailing at the time would surely have influenced the character of Alexander's 'reasoned' approach to his ongoing explorations. In his book, 'Use of the Self', he says, '*when I began my investigation, I, in common with most people, conceived of 'body' and 'mind' as separate parts of the same organism,*' but his experience of teaching gradually taught him that '*it is impossible to separate mental and physical processes in any form of human activity.*'

By Alexander's time, Western cultural and historical ideas of separation of mind and body, Cartesian dualism, had considerably weakened. But his recognition of 'psycho-physical unity' — which encompassed the broad principle that mind, body, emotions and spirit were interdependent — was both radical and original at the end of the 19th century.

# Chapter 2
# Alexander Technique Skills

## Underlying Principles

This chapter describes the classic Alexander skills of maintaining 'primary freedom', 'inhibition' and 'giving directions'. The later chapter, *The Alchemy of Alexander,* has a more contemporary focus on holistic personal development that goes beyond the concept of learning a 'technique' as such, and includes sections on *Expanded Attention* and *Skilled Alexander Touch.*

The Technique can be described as a gradual process of re-education, concerned with developing more awareness of how we move or come to rest, and of how we habitually respond to situations or various stimuli. We learn to notice our subtle patterns of contraction, of muscle, mind, emotions, or spirit. This learning process is facilitated by skilled hands-on work with a teacher.

One of F M Alexander's crucial discoveries was his recognition of *psycho-physical unity*, that subtle relationship between mind and muscle, how minds and bodies involve each other; he often used the phrase, *'use of the self'* to express this unity. Neuroscience now refers to the idea of 'embodied cognition.'

He also emphasised the importance of only employing those

muscles which were needed, '*getting out of the way of natural good use*' or '*not interfering with natural good use of ourselves*', which refers to an inner intelligence, an innate drive to health and equilibrium. In time, the natural good functioning and freedom of movement that most of us had as small children can resurface. We can also 're-member' the relationship of our limbs to our backs and appreciate the radically different character and functioning of our arms and legs, as we explore how to fine-tune the degree of muscular effort required for a particular activity.

Students gradually improve their body sense or kinaesthesia. They learn to recognise a feeling of wellbeing, of spaciousness and lightness, of having room to breathe, which invites a quality of openness to their thoughts and feelings.

Many people initially come to Alexander for help with musculoskeletal pain, breathing problems, chronic physical/mental health issues. Professional performers of any kind are likely to find this training invaluable for their profession, but Alexander also increases appreciation and even enjoyment of our astonishingly wide repertoire and combinations of every-day movements. We can expand, contract, crawl, run, crouch, jump, collapse, relax, release, twist, bend, stretch, lift, push, pull, etc.

\*\*\*

The photograph below is of a five-year-old who is still young enough to enjoy his birthright of a spacious and co-ordinated, 'natural good use of himself'. His head, neck, trunk alignment (primary freedom) is working well while he is focussed on a demanding activity. Neither he nor his teacher are familiar with the Alexander Technique!

# Primary Freedom (Primary Control)

The word 'control' can now have misleading, rather rigid overtones so I have used the phrase 'primary freedom', as it better conveys the spacious, dynamic quality required.

\*\*\*

*But they obeyed not, neither inclined their ear, but made their neck stiff that they might not hear nor receive instruction.*

*King James Bible — Jeremiah 17.23*

\*\*\*

F M Alexander recognised that the subtle, mobile relationship between head, neck and back, which he called 'the primary control', had a profound effect on the functioning and coordination of the entire body and he referred to this relationship as, *'no less than our primordial inheritance as vertebrates'.* Being a keen horseman, he may have had this rather original realisation as he watched horses race, or jump over gates, and noticed how the horses' heads led their bodies in a coordinated manner, with their spines lengthening as they ran. We can easily visualise this sinuous, elastic movement in other quadrupeds.

Don Burton said that:

*the ultimate skill we are teaching people is to leave themselves alone enough, in a variety of situations and stimuli, so that our*

> *primary freedom works well and therefore the rest of the body follows. Freeing the head and neck region improves the balance, coordination and muscle tone of the entire body.*

When asked if paying attention to the primary freedom was enough, he also said, '*no, ...ultimately, yes*' — by which he meant that adult students' physical, emotional and psychological blocks often presented very real difficulties in re-establishing reliable primary freedom for quite some time.

The working of primary freedom in a human being is a delicate balancing  mechanism, easily interfered with by tension elsewhere. It can best be seen in the coordinated, graceful movements of young children who move easily in a way seldom seen in adults.

The confident, fluid drawing below, by a three-year-old, may show an awareness of necks.

The skull, which weighs five kilos on average, balances on the atlas, the top vertebra of the spine. Tiny but crucial muscles round both atlas and axis, the second vertebra, feed information back to the brain, and the brain stem is a major neural pathway between brain and body. There are deep muscles in the nape of the neck which regulate muscle tone and posture throughout the body. Important stretch reflexes in the neck are elicited by the natural balance of the head in relation to a lengthened and supported spine.

An open nape of the neck also helps the yoke of the shoulders, or shoulder girdle (formed by shoulder blades and collar bones) to rest onto the ribs. The armpits then relax, the shoulder blades drop down the back and the chest becomes more spacious, all of which improve breathing. Many of us will have noticed how easily our emotions and thoughts affect our neck and shoulders, and hence our breathing!

\*\*\*

**John Hunter**, Alexander teacher, brings this whole complex area to life with the following inspiring comment from his blog:

> *The freedom of the atlanto-occipital joint and the tone of the sub-occipital muscles are intricately connected with mental and emotional states. The point at which the base of the skull sits on the atlas can be thought of as not only the physical connection between head and spine, but also the place where mind and body interface; a two-way flow of information and feedback. Sensitive hands can detect subtle energies flowing through this area. These energies relate to and are influenced by mental and emotional processes.*

\*\*\*

Remarkably, the neck may move as much as 600 times an hour; it is often in constant motion as it supports and moves the head, movements initiated by our intentions, by our thoughts and emotions and by what comes to our attention and to our senses, such as the smell of burning or a sudden noise. Our necks are a barometer of stress so the thought of inviting an open, 'out of gear' quality can help us to 'leave our necks alone' rather than trying to 'do' something with them. The same applies to the 'little necks' of our ankles and wrists...

\*\*\*

In Western culture, adults often tend to stiffen their necks but in Fiji (a group of islands in the South Pacific) necks can apparently be quite expressive:

> *Watching people listen was even better. There was a lovely widely shared mannerism that I couldn't recall seeing before: a slight, jerky shifting of the head from side to side; a constant cocking of the neck, notch by notch, the way a bird does. I read it as a gesture of extreme tolerance. The listener was continually resetting his mind at different angles in order to take in different speakers, different impressions with maximum equanimity.*

> **William Finnegan:** *Barbarian Days — a surfing life.* 2015

# Inhibition

*Everything can be taken from a man but one thing: the last of the human freedoms — to choose one's attitude in any given set of circumstances, to choose one's own way. Between stimulus and response there is a space. In that space is our power to choose our response. In our response lies our growth and our freedom.*

**Victor E Frankl**: *Man's Search for Meaning.* 2004 (1946 in German)

\*\*\*

The skill of 'inhibition' is about *not getting ahead of oneself* and is central to the Technique. It concerns the ability to pause, to take time to notice what is happening, to 'recollect' oneself, in both a cognitive and sensory manner.

It may involve reconsidering responses to a stimulus or situation, whatever that might be. Included in this concept is *not end-gaining*, not trying to fix problems, not being focussed on getting results, but seeing to the moment-by-moment *means whereby* (Alexander's phrases).

Inhibition can be understood as a state of open-minded readiness, (like a car being out of gear), in which one is aware of a stimulus, does not deny or blank it out, but which prevents the brain from triggering neural activity, and therefore muscular activity as a consequence. When we feel called upon to act, to 'get ready', we are likely to trigger a reflex which contracts the back and buttock muscles and arches the spine.

The skill of 'inhibition' gives us a chance, a choice, not to activate this neuromuscular response.

Don Burton understood inhibition, in essence, as a meditative process, a *deep neurological stopping,* to allow a sense of inner spaciousness to arise. He thought that Alexander's idea of inhibition was to allow enough time to get in touch with our own sense of well-being, to find a place of trust in the body, *so that whatever happened next came from a place that was better organised.*

To pause and to 'take enough time to get in touch with our sense of our own well-being' goes against much of modern urban living but, in the longer term, this skill, or new habit, can be immensely valuable and pleasurable in day-to-day life, as well as in the more specific contexts of creative enquiry or sporting performance.

\*\*\*

Both 'inhibiting' and 'directing' are F M Alexander's phrases that have specific meanings in an Alexander context. His use of the word 'inhibition' did not have the overtones that it has now, since Freud's (1856-1939) use of the word. Initially, the idea of inhibition can sometimes be misunderstood as pulling ourselves up short and becoming nervous of habitual spontaneous responses! This may create an aura of restraint in students which was not what Alexander intended.

He loved the theatre and would have recognised that 'waiting in the wings' (where actors wait behind the scenes to go on stage) was an opportunity to align body and mind, taking time to get ready. Many actors, musicians and other performance artists will be familiar with the Technique, and will have learnt to become aware of and 'inhibit' their tendency to get ahead of themselves, as they anticipate performing. They may notice, for example, the early signs of nervous system activation such as an increased heart rate, sweating, or shallow breathing and muscular tension.

Once they are on stage, actors, comedians and other performance artists know the crucial importance of timing, giving phrases or movements time to breathe; the same is true for music. Miles Davis, the great jazz artist, said, *'it's not the notes you play, it's the notes you don't play'*. This discernment can also be understood as a form of inhibition.

\*\*\*

## A few examples of situations that involve inhibition:

Not 'jumping the gun' at the start of a race

A footballer preparing to take a penalty

Waiting to cross the road or at traffic lights

Pausing before replying, during conversation

Not planning one's own response while listening to someone else

Any performance artist or public speaker 'taking time to breathe'

Not making premature assumptions about other people

An adult animal can keep completely still while stalking its prey, while young animals that haven't yet learnt to hold back, rush in prematurely.

*\*\*\**

There are certain circumstances when inhibition, which may be orchestrated by the higher brain, the pre-frontal cortex, would be inappropriate. Our instinctive, hard-wired, much older reptilian brain's responses to perceived danger are not normally in our control, and elicit an instant response of fight, flight or freeze to danger or threat, such as being surprised by a predatory animal, or seeing a child run into the road.

# Directing

F M Alexander understood 'giving directions' as a cognitive activity emanating from the pre-frontal cortex, like turning on a light in the area above the eyes. He did not think that this process was dependent on paying attention to incoming sensory information or involved 'doing' anything, but that it made changes in the body by waking up neural pathways in the brain. In practice, there is inevitably an interweaving of sensory and motor information, although sensory information travels more slowly.

*The purpose of consciously directing thoughts in this way is to enliven spatial thinking, and to act as a preventative, to counteract many people's habitual tendency to narrow and pull down.*

A simplified way of exploring 'directing' is to take attention into the space all around and above the body, using the mind to invite expansion and a sense of subtle movement and connection throughout the whole system. Hand can release from elbow, elbow from shoulder blades, sacrum and tailbone from back of head (occiput bone), toes from heels...

F M Alexander's classic instructions for 'directing' were of having the thought, the intention, the suggestion to the body, *to let the neck be free, to let the head go forward and up (ie, not tilted back) in such a way that the back can lengthen and widen (including widening across the shoulders), knees out and away.* Giving the direction *back and up* for the neck and head is also useful for those who tend to poke their heads forward, an increasingly common habit from using smart phones/computer screens.

He felt that the use of imagery while giving directions, or during other aspects of practice, could be distracting and muddy clarity of thought. There is also the contemporary issue that we are frequently bombarded with imagery, so our visual faculties can be over-stimulated and our capacity to stay present reduced.

Some teachers use a different vocabulary for directing. How students understand or are taught to employ directing can be quite an individual matter, and this may change as they gain more experience of the intricacies of how their mind affects their body and vice versa. Directing can eventually become something that happens by itself. It is like a fluid pulse of intelligence moving through the system from a body memory of previous experience of directing.

*\*\*\**

For many teachers and students, working with the flow of subtle energy, 'qi', or 'chi', is part of their understanding and experience of Alexander, even if some would not express it in this way. Damo Mitchell, director of Lotus Nei Gong School of Eastern Energy Arts, has made some useful comments about how the flow of subtle energy in the body is influenced by the mind.

Although he speaks from a different discipline, I have included some of his comments here because the language he uses is a helpful, more poetic complement to Alexander's language. Alexander does refer to directing energy in the body, but I doubt if he would go along with Damo's approach; relaxation was not a word he would have used, which he associated with slumping.

> *Listening with your mind to your body is not the same as listening with your ears. Mind will begin to melt into the body and flow like a fluid through the entire system. The more you relax the mind the more it is led through your body, like fluid soaking into a sponge.*

**Damo Mitchell:** *A Comprehensive Guide to Daoist Nei Gong.* 2018

\*\*\*

Of particular interest is Peter Grunwald's discovery that every single area of the visual system corresponds with an associated area in the body. For example, the thought of expanding widthways and lengthways across the cornea, the surface of the eye, helps to open the chest and also subtly changes the experience of what we see. If the visual system slumps and narrows, so does the structure of the body. This can be an issue with prolonged computer use and with wearing glasses.

**Peter Grunwald:** *Eye Body: the art of integrating eye, brain and body.* 2008

# Chapter 3
## Coming to our Senses

## Kinaesthesia and Other Senses

Many Alexander students find that they are 'out of touch with themselves' and need to 'come to their senses'. They gradually reclaim their body sense or kinaesthetic sense, a collection of senses that can refer to *somatic, internal experience, both in motion and at rest.*

As they become more present and open to the subtle effects of skilled Alexander touch, they are also likely to become more receptive to sensory feedback from their surroundings, to the sounds of urban or rural soundscapes, to the smell of rain falling on dry ground, or the smell of geranium leaves, to see with fresh eyes...

Over 2000 years ago, Aristotle listed only five senses: sight, sound, smell, taste and touch. He saw that all these senses allowed us to receive and interpret, as reliably as possible, information or stimulus coming from *outside ourselves*, from our environment, that was relevant for our survival. A noticeable omission from Aristotle's list are the kinaesthetic senses.

The word kinaesthesia (Greek origin) and the word proprioception (Latin origin) both came into use in the 19th century. Like many words in the English language, there are subtle differences in how we understand them but in practice they are often used interchangeably. The word 'proprioception' might be used more for our ability to orientate ourselves in space. Kinaesthesia is, perhaps, a broader term, often related to movement. This sense is also involved in a more general monitoring and maintenance of posture and muscle tone, the sense of our own weight and, ultimately, of our substance. It is also intimately tied up with self-awareness and 'inner knowing', which includes intuitive knowledge coming from the heart or from a 'gut' level. We now know about the enteric nervous system, the sheaths of millions of neurons identical to brain tissue, which are embedded in the walls of the gut from oesophagus to anus.

One way of tuning into kinaesthetic sensation is to explore *slow*, floppy rolling on the floor, with arms above the head, allowing gravity to do the work. This requires a luxurious, languorous, smiling quality.... and is a rare example of spiralic movement not initiated by the head but more by the elbows or knees, hands and feet which lead the torso.

*** 

There is now huge debate about the number and character of our senses, a discussion amplified by the new discipline of neuroscience. No sense operates in isolation, and they are all tinged with memory, emotions, thoughts and imagination. Our senses work together.

The following quotation is from science fiction, but our sense of smell and, importantly, our imagination, registers its impact.

> *...the unmistakable smell of the Sprawl, a rich amalgam of stale subway exhalations, ancient soot and the carcinogenic tang of fresh plastics, all of it shot through with the carbon edge of illicit fossil fuels...*

**William Gibson:** *Count Zero.* 1986

\*\*\*

We know, in far more detail than in Alexander's time, that our nervous system receives a great deal of sensory input from inside our bodies, particularly from our myofascial tissues. Feedback is also provided by muscle spindles, specialised stretch receptors attached to muscle fibres. When a muscle is stretched, this change in length is transmitted to the spindles. Current research suggests that sensory information from muscle spindles is more important than that coming from joints and is integrated by the central nervous system.

\*\*\*

Kathryn Linn Geurts discovered that the five-senses model has little relevance for the Anlo-Ewe-speaking people in southeast Ghana who value and prioritise their sense of 'seselelame' (literally feel-feel-at-flesh-inside) and she comments that most Americans would not even identify this as a sense.*

***

When students first start Alexander sessions, their subjective perception of how they habitually move and respond to stimulus of any kind is likely to be 'unreliable' and blunted but this will change, over a period of time, to become more accurate, as their kinaesthetic sense and other senses gradually become more finely tuned.

F M Alexander knew that someone with a chronically over-tensed neck and shoulders could report that they felt 'relaxed and normal'. He observed that his habitual use of his whole body felt 'familiar and therefore right,' despite evidence to the contrary, which he could see in a mirror. He referred to this distorted self-perception as 'unreliable sensory appreciation', or by the rather intriguing phrase 'debauched kinaesthesia.'

Michael Bloch, in his biography of Alexander, comments that, '*one often feels that debauched kinaesthesia occupies the same role in Alexander's view of the world as sin does in an evangelical Christian view of the world*' — Alexander's background was indeed staunchly evangelical Protestant.

***

* **Kathryn Linn Geurts**: *Culture and the Senses — bodily ways of knowing in an African community.* UCP 2002 (extract from synopsis on the net).

Neuro-linguistic programming (NLP) makes the important point that people's dominant mode for processing information can significantly differ, either by natural inclination or force of circumstance.

The preferred mode might be predominantly auditory, visual, kinaesthetic or mental. This pre-disposition will also be likely to influence which aspects of Alexander work particularly interest individuals.

For some people, the loss or alteration of one or more of the senses can be life-changing and radically affect their sense of self. However, there are many inspiring examples of how individuals have responded. The Scottish virtuoso percussionist Dame Evelyn Glennie, profoundly deaf since the age of twelve, has refined her body's receptivity to the vibrational qualities of her instruments to a very high degree.

Chris Downey, US architect, abruptly lost his sight in his mid-forties but he is now a multi-sensory designer who assesses acoustics, touch and airflow of urban spaces to make them more welcoming. He says, '*I was fascinated walking through buildings that I knew (when I was sighted), but I was experiencing them in a different way... I was hearing the architecture, feeling the space.*'

Some of those at the high-functioning end of the autistic[*] spectrum experience the world mainly through sound. Studies

* **Temple Grandin**: *The Autistic Brain*. 2014.

of autism have neglected sensory issues but sensory over-sensitivity can be very debilitating for some autistic people whilst only a mild difficulty for others.

\*\*\*

There are people who seek out extreme sports as a route to stimulating sensory feeling and heightened awareness of living in the present moment. These same activities also attract a wide range of enthusiasts who deeply appreciate the zen-like experiences these activities bring to what many would call a spiritual path.

I have become interested in reading a variety of surfers' and climbers' accounts of how they experience an activity that offers, or perhaps demands, the supreme opportunity for perfect motion, perfect 'use of themselves' and, above all, acute multi-sensory awareness. They must maintain their attention over a wide range of personal and environmental information, 'expanding their library of movement skills', as their lives may depend on it.

*The focus required to climb to my limit seemed to heighten my senses. The contrasts in the rock would jump out at me. I would notice things like the sweet smell of juniper in the wind. I was more aware of the rhythm of my breath and the preciseness of my body movements. We would climb every day, testing ourselves and expanding our library of movement skills on different types of rock... each time I felt strong, lighter, more skillful than the last.*

**Tommy Caldwell** (elite US climber)*The Push— a climber's journey of endurance, risk and going beyond limits. 2017.
Also see YouTube — The Dawn Wall.*

\*\*\*

The extraordinary, multi-faceted, Portuguese poet **Fernando Pessoa** (1888–1935) wrote in a number of different 'voices' and languages.

in the voice or heteronym of Alberto Campero

### I'm a keeper of sheep

*I'm a keeper of sheep.*
*The sheep are my thoughts*
*and my thoughts are all sensations.*
*I think with my eyes and ears*
*and with my hands and feet*
*and with my nose and mouth.*

*To think a flower is to see it and smell it*
*and to eat a fruit is to taste its meaning.*
*That's why on a hot day,*
*when I ache from enjoying it so much,*
*and stretch out on the grass,*
*closing my warm eyes,*
*I feel my whole body lying full length in reality.*
*I know the truth and am happy.*

**Fernando Pessoa**: *Poems of Fernando Pessoa*. 1998.
Extract from a much longer poem 'The Keeper of Sheep', stanza IX.

34

## Kinaesthetic Dystonia

'Kinaesthetic dystonia' or 'sensory-motor amnesia' refers to the loss or partial loss of the ability to listen to and be informed by the body, a distortion or reduction of conscious awareness of muscular activity, internal sensations or those of touch.

Over time, some people may gradually develop protective layers of tight muscle which can dull their emotions and reduce their kinaesthetic awareness, both of which may affect their ability to be present. They may become unaware of how much this can affect their health or how they interact with others, what is draining for them and what might be restorative.

Despite a culture obsessed by the body and by appearance, many adults are deeply out of touch with their bodies, especially in contemporary urban societies dominated by technology, and may admit to being too busy in their heads, or having too much mental clutter.

There are many reasons why some people appear to have shut down sensations of touch or of kinaesthesia. This may have roots in long-term habitual ways of using their bodies, from repetitive strain, or it may be the result of long term cultural/ societal influences. A friend, who was educated in a school run by nuns, was taught to ignore bodily signals such as being cold or hungry. Her mother, educated in the same school, had a similar approach. As a result, this friend, as an adult, tends to discount her experiences of physical or emotional discomfort.

Kinaesthetic dystonia may also arise from physical or emotional trauma. One of the body's primal impulses when faced with stressful or traumatic events is to contract/dissociate as a protective response.

We have a very ancient reptilian brain above the top of the spinal cord which controls basic bodily functions and a mammalian or limbic brain, deep in the middle of the brain which governs emotions and beliefs. Our much more recently evolved neo-cortex, which is about 80% of our brains, is concerned with processing many different types of information, including that from the senses. The complex relationship between these different parts of our brains, each reacting in different ways to the effects of a traumatic event, can make it more difficult for us to process trauma than for other animals.

# Chapter 4
# Alchemy of the Alexander Technique

## A Process of Transformation

*Alchemy — a medieval forerunner of chemistry concerned with the transmutation of base metal into gold or finding the universal elixir of immortality...*

✳✳✳

The Alexander Technique could be described as an art form, an exploratory process, which changes people's perception of themselves as they gain an increased inner awareness and also learn to experience the world around them with fresh eyes — the core of much artistic activity.

Many artists (and maybe some Alexander teachers) would say that that their habitual mode of processing information tends to be more 'right brained' — with reference to the right hemisphere of the brain, which may be conducive to a more intuitive, holistic and imaginative approach.

For more information on the complex topic of the divided brain, see this seminal and influential book:

**Iain McGilchrist**, *The Master and his Emissary — the divided brain and the making of the Western world.* YUP 2010.

✳✳✳

One of Alexander's important strengths is that it gives time for a recalibration of a student's whole system and beliefs about themselves. These changes are likely to highlight, or cast a new light on, their emotional and physical history, so they may be surprised by the emotional or psychic impact of this training, in addition to their cognitive understanding.

Over a period of time, students come to recognise a sense of interconnected energy flow within their whole body and a solid, supported, grounded presence, a feeling of being embodied, if Alexander is taught well. This ideally gives a safe container within which the process of transformation can take place so they can begin to process/release stress and trauma and do emotional work on themselves.

Many students may appear superficially open but their underlying concerns, their physical and emotional history, their attitudes and their stories about themselves are unlikely to be apparent. If students are too 'armoured', uncoordinated or ungrounded, there is a real danger that the Technique can become an externally imposed prescriptive set of instructions, a papering over the cracks.

The word 'technique' can be a misnomer as it tends to limit perception of the depth of work that Alexander can offer. The skills of the Technique as such are perfectly valid but can also be understood as a window to the full potential of this work to offer deep personal change, in the longer term.

\*\*\*

These brief accounts may help to bring the potentially transformative nature of Alexander more to life. The subsequent sections, *Skilled Alexander Touch* and *Expanded Attention* also give more detail.

> *I can still recall the intensity of my first experience of the Alexander Technique in March 1978. Although nothing dramatic seemed to happen during the lesson — and from the outside the untrained eye might think nothing was happening — the changes in my nervous system were profound. After the session, which lasted no more than twenty-five minutes, I went to a nearby café to drink a cup of coffee and try to process the new sensations, which I can best describe as awareness of myself as a living organism rather than as a continuously changing procession of thoughts.*

**John Hunter:** Alexander teacher

\*\*\*

*I had a sense of actually living in my physical body instead of being constantly removed through nervous anticipation and self criticism... So often the mind can grasp at the possibility of change quite quickly but the nervous system and the tissues need much more time and experience to begin to embody the new possibility and make it our own.*

**Margaret Edis:** Alexander teacher — interviewed by David Clark.
*StatNews*, Sept 1996

\*\*\*

*I was watching, observing and listening to myself more often. I reacted a bit less to pain, had less lower back pain and felt much better... I felt that this experience could challenge people's belief system about themselves.*

**Judit Pasztor**: Alexander student, now an Alexander teacher

\*\*\*

*I had a very real feeling of coming back to some place I had already been. At a corporeal level Alexander seemed very different from my previous experiences of yoga and Pilates because it gave me a feeling of wholeness. In the case of yoga, you still need to 'combine' two things: body and mind. I have never before experienced that feeling of unity with my body and mind and somehow having access to it.*

**Aleksandra**: translator

# Skilled Alexander Touch

One of the unique aspects of Alexander is the transformative power of skilled hand contact from a teacher. A teacher's hands can reflect students back to themselves and clarify their capacity to notice more clearly what they are doing or thinking. They may say, '*I didn't realise how my thoughts were affecting my neck and how I held my breath.*'

\*\*\*

*I would feel, as his hands first came on me, an immediate amplification of my own sense of myself. My deep underlying pattern of my use of myself would come more clearly into my consciousness. And yet there was also an underlying feeling tone of: it's ok to be who you are.*

**John Nicholls:** Alexander teacher. Extract from his contribution to 'Remembering Walter Carrington', who died in 2005

\*\*\*

Alexander teachers can also convey something of the qualities of their own 'use of themselves' to their students, via hands-on work. They can transmit a subtle blueprint of the quality of freedom in their own systems. A teacher can also sense to what extent students are able to 'listen' to that hand contact and are able to monitor their own 'use of themselves'.

It can seem like part of an exploratory 'dance' of two people working together, following the breath, allowing bodily, emotional, mental or subtle energy shifts to show the way, and enable students to begin to let go of habitual patterns of mental and physical stress.

This quiet, 'non-doing' touch re-awakens the subtle relationship between mind and muscle. Students gradually learn to take their own internal echo soundings, to find an inner compass and experience a new or more authentic sense of self. They may say they feel witnessed at a deep level, akin to some forms of counselling.

\*\*\*

The hands are rich in sensory nerve endings; the fingertips have the highest amount of nerve proprioceptors of any area of the body so they are acutely sensitive to even the most minute of impulses and variations in  muscle activity and subtle energy flow. We may use computers or tools, write, drive, cook, clean, open a door, wash, cradle a baby... Our hands are part of how we shape our everyday world.

F M Alexander did not originally use his hands at all in his teaching of others. He believed that he could simply explain what he had discovered to his students, but this proved to have serious limitations! At some point he realised that he would also have to show his students what he meant, and so the Technique then became a hands-on method. Over the years he refined the use of his hands. Later in his teaching career he said, *'my brain is in my hands. ...it is demonstrable... except that you should be conscious of the experience you acquire under the direction of my hands.'*

Michael Bloch, Alexander's biographer, makes the interesting comment that a number of people who worked with Alexander confirmed that, although he was highly skilled at changing a person's 'use of themselves' for the better, *'he had no idea who the person was that he was touching'*. He adds that this propensity exists today in the larger Alexander community, hence Don Burton's comment to trainee teachers, *'when you put hands on, put them on the whole person.'*

\*\*\*

Miranda Tufnell had many sessions with Bill Williams who had trained with F M Alexander. She subsequently trained as an Alexander teacher with Don Burton.

*Working with Bill Williams taught me to be still, to notice and track the moment by moment shifts and interplay of thought in my body. Through his lessons I sensed the subtle yet enormous shifts of qualities that occur in all of us — we can soften, freeze, harden, float, collapse — all in an instant according to what we encounter and how we place our attention. I think of Bill Williams as my first real dance teacher. He had originally been in the Air Force and had trained with Alexander himself. He taught me to listen to my body and to sense in this stillness a cascade of many kinds of movement — thoughts, feelings, memories, sensations — his touch anchored me and gave me a map through which to sift perceptions — to notice what I was doing moment by moment, in mind and body. I remember how the delicacy and lightness of his touch enabled me to experience not just my shoulder or neck, but my whole body, and in an entirely new way. Bill worked with his eyes closed, constantly accompanying his touch with a running stream of directions… I feel that Bill taught me to come home to myself.*

**Miranda Tufnell**

Dance artist, cranio-sacral therapist and Alexander teacher

# Expanded Attention

This section is describing a particular skill developed during Alexander sessions which can also apply to anyone's daily lives. It can also apply through time — with memory, anticipation, imagination...

A specific, day-to-day example of expanded attention is that of learning to drive, when our attention is likely to be stretched, or rather, over-stretched, between the many aspects of driving a vehicle: the various sounds of the engine, the mechanics of driving, travel conditions and regulations, a possible fellow passenger and our own thoughts and emotions, at least until the habitual patterns of driving behaviour have become established.

Another example is learning to play an instrument, which may involve a similar 'over-stretched' experience. A player may be employing Alexander skills, and perhaps noticing their physical and emotional state, while also being in relationship to their instrument, and to the acoustic space, and to their possible audience. Maybe they are also reading music or listening to a teacher and to their own musical efforts. As any player knows, the ability to keep a spacious awareness of this spectrum of expanded attention takes quite a while to learn.

\*\*\*

The following quotation encapsulates this quality of expanded attention in more expressive language:

> *The Alexander Technique freed me from the hamster wheel of my thoughts and worries by refining my awareness of my own body, whilst also opening up my perception of what was around me — it taught me to breathe more fully in my body and also in my attention — to notice the nuance of detail within me whilst expanding, widening my field of attention to include the world about me. This helps me to feel connected to what is around me and thus to orient myself in my life.*

**Miranda Tufnell**
Dance artist, cranio-sacral therapist and Alexander teacher

\*\*\*

An awareness of how we shift or expand our attention is on a spectrum, ranging from noticing our internal, kinaesthetic sensations and our thoughts through to being aware of our complex interactions with the world around us. The quality and focus of our attention will be endlessly fluctuating and fluid. Conscious, humorous or rueful recognition of this aspect of Alexander is very much part of the skills involved. F M Alexander's phrase *'thinking in activity'* partly relates to the skill of developing this expanded field of awareness. It can be quite a juggling act!

The difficulty lies in maintaining a balance between our awareness of our internal and external environment. We may be able to retain some degree of our sense of ourselves, our own energy field, how we are moving, our use of Alexander skills, but we may lose this awareness when we start to pay attention to what is happening around us, or when interacting with other people.

\*\*\*

During an Alexander session, students learn to give particular attention to their backs and to the space behind them, around them, above their heads, and to the ground beneath their feet. They may find that, by expanding their attention in this way, they are also more able to notice the peripheral, sensory, aesthetic, or cognitive aspects of their physical surroundings: the views, sounds, smells, movement, atmosphere, temperature, qualities of space, light and colour in the room or in the landscape. They learn to be more aware of how they move in relationship to their surroundings and to other people.

\*\*\*

This remarkable ability to monitor the range and quality of our attention, at least to some degree, is an innate survival skill. Those people still living relatively traditional lifestyles across the world are likely to be on the alert for changes in their natural environment: the sounds, smells, bird, human and animal behaviour, as they keep an intuitive, 'weather eye' out for threats to their livelihood or to themselves — a state of relaxed alertness close to mindfulness. (Parents of small children also learn to 'keep a weather eye open', even in their sleep...).

However, an increasing number of people are now less attentive to this survival skill, oblivious of their immediate environment while using mobile phones or headphones... Working in small rooms or feeling cramped in a city environment may also influence the ability to expand attention while staying grounded.

***

A shepherd from the North York moors once came to see me because he had strained his back muscles carrying a sheep and knew he was 'out of true'. I had the impression that his long experience of scanning the wide-open expanses of the moors and skies had become part of his sense of himself, and of the quality of his attention. He stays in my mind as that rare example of a Western adult with excellent kinaesthetic sense, who was also imbued with a deep awareness and knowledgeable appreciation of his surroundings.

***

A particular session with Don Burton during my own teacher training remains vividly in my mind and body memory.

I was standing with outstretched arms in front of a window looking out to the Cumbrian hills. Don was standing behind me, with one hand on the side of my ribs and his other hand reaching round my back to my solar plexus. As I relaxed the outer layers of my body, my whole trunk expanded; my breathing seemed to connect all four limbs into my back and into the space around me. I also felt that my auric, or subtle energy field was expanding.

He asked me to look up to the hill-tops and to stay with my sense of myself while using my imagination to take my attention down through the hills and then tracing a circuit to underneath my feet and back up through my body to my eyes, while still focussing on the hill-tops. I felt that we were articulating the space between teacher and student, between us and the landscape, between how I felt inside myself and my awareness of sensory information coming from outside myself. The ability to expand my attention, yet stay with a spacious awareness within myself, seemed to work together.

# Chapter 5
# Our Bipedal Inheritance

## Being a Biped

The distinctive human habit of walking upright was a major transformation in human evolution, and an appreciation of both the complexity and vulnerability of our bipedal functioning is integral to many aspects of Alexander.

\*\*\*

How bipeds balance is a crucial part of our inheritance, with far-reaching implications for what it means 'to be balanced'. This is part of our feeling of being present in and aware of our surrounding, of our balance in the wider sense of the word. Balance and listening are very closely related. We can of course become 'unbalanced' and fall.

Kathryn Linn Geurts has studied the senses of the Anlo-Ewe people in south-east Ghana.* She says that children growing up in this culture learn that balance is an essential component of what it means to be human, where balance is a sense (in a physical and psychological sense, as well as in literal and

---

* **Kathryn Linn Geurts**: *Culture and the Senses — bodily ways of knowing in an African community*. UCP 2002 (extract from synopsis on the net).

metaphorical ways). A person's balance shows up in the way they stand, the way they walk and the way they carry themselves through life; it expresses who they are in a fundamental way.

Children grasp something of their bipedal inheritance at an early age. The drawing above is by a five-year-old.

If we balance on one leg, (the other leg just touching the floor with the forefoot or big toe, if needed), arms stretched out while relaxing our shoulders, we may notice how every part of our body is subtly adjusting to refine our balance and coordination; large muscles in the back, extensor muscles, expand when we are upright, to help our balance. This stance is also an excellent way of clarifying our sense of how each part of our bodies affects the rest.

*** 

Our bipedal systems are designed for a very wide range of movement  rather than for standing or sitting still for any length of time. We are uniquely well adapted to run for long distances, which doubtless helped our ancestors to survive.

Runners may say that they find the Technique useful and enjoyable, that it helps speed and stamina, and improves their breathing. They learn to keep their attention in the present moment, not to 'end-gain' (get ahead of themselves) and to keep 'expanded attention' — awareness of the space and the environment around them, while monitoring how they are in themselves.

Losing body hair and having a large number of sweat glands has allowed us to sweat more easily and stay cool in the heat. Our strong Achilles tendons at the back of our ankles, and our buttock muscles, are also essential for long-distance running. In common with dogs and horses, we have a long nuchal ligament from the back of our skulls to the base of our necks which stabilises our heads as we move. In addition, the three ligamentous arches that we have in each foot, plus fat pads in the heels, all act as shock absorbers.

In a very moving and powerful sequence, David Attenborough has filmed a group of San people engaged in an uniquely human activity — the skill of 'persistence hunting'.* They are following the spoor of a kudu in the Kalahari Desert and take eight hours to run it down to the point of exhaustion; unlike bipeds, quadrupeds cannot run long distances in the heat without overheating, although many are far faster than us for shorter distances.

***

During our evolution, the alignment of our head to our body shifted and our spine developed the significant, uniquely human, counter-balanced series of flexible curves which absorb the impact of our feet, taking the weight of our bodies as we move.

Our ability to support ourselves against gravity without bracing or stiffening our joints enables us to freely adjust every area of our bodies, with a puppet-like flexibility, so that we may move more easily over uneven ground.

We do not have to hold ourselves up. Part of our bipedal blueprint is an anti-gravity postural reflex which creates a buoyant quality, a ricochet effect up through the body, like bouncing a ball. Paradoxically, this reflex encourages the torso to hang freely from the skull, albeit with the support of fascia and ligaments.

It is important that this 'up' quality, emphasised in Alexander practice, is counter-balanced by an awareness of the

---

* **David Attenborough**: *Life of Mammals*. BBC — 10th episode, first series 2002.

grounding energy of the belly, the weight of the pelvis and sacrum, and the crucial connection to the ground through legs and feet.

\*\*\*

*I had an opportunity to truly drop into my pelvis and let my legs drop away from my hip joints. I had the sense that I had found my centre and freedom from there. This was probably the first time I understood that standing up without holding myself anywhere in any way is not only possible but natural.... I had not realised that if we allowed everything to drop down, muscle tension would release. It made me feel lengthened and widened, spacious.*

**Judit Pasztor**
Student at SEAS training school, now an Alexander teacher

\*\*\*

The fascia, ligaments and tendons, plus our muscles and skeleton, all work together as a lattice-work of support, converting the whole system into a spring-like framework.

A useful analogy is the interdependent structures at work in a geodesic dome, a principle described by the American architect Buckminster Fuller as 'tensegrity'. Our bones act as spacers and more weight is borne by the connective tissue than by the bony beams of the skeleton. This complex network bears most of the responsibility for providing a stable upright posture and graceful carriage.

\*\*\*

By learning to balance on two feet and walk upright, we have been able to extend our range of vision and free up our hands for making and using tools, for preparing and obtaining food more effectively. We are more versatile with our hands than any other creature on the planet and have gained a remarkably wide range of both gross and fine motor skills.

The evolution of our cerebral cortex has enabled us to stand back from the world, from ourselves and from the immediacy of our experience, which has helped us to plan, to think flexibly and inventively. Our adaptability has enabled us to survive as a species.

\*\*\*

The photograph below shows two classic bipedal postures — a Western adult still able to drop into a full squat, and the open, upright carriage of his son, whose head is beautifully poised on top of his spine. Full, bare-foot squatting relaxes the soles of the feet which enables us to feel more connected into the earth. It also encourages the spine to lengthen and relieves compression in the lumbar and sacral areas. This default posture, in the absence of chairs, is, of course, in common use in many parts of the world.

Quadrupeds are likely to retain the full length of their spines and, for the most part, their spiralic movements until old age. But for many of us, especially in more urban societies, there is, too often, a gradual progression from a young child's flexible poise and openness to the habitually pulled-down, tense or disconnected appearance of an increasing number of teenagers and adults. Bipeds are at far more risk than quadrupeds from the many influences that collapse, brace or otherwise distort and override our naturally buoyant bipedal framework, including injuries from falling.

\*\*\*

It can be useful to remember that our skeletons are not fixed but are changing all the time, although less so as we get older.

*We used to view our skeletons primarily as a mechanical structure, as scaffolding for the rest of the body but bones are live organs which produce a protein hormone called osteocalcin which is now believed to play a role in regulating a whole range of vital bodily processes such as memory, muscle health and metabolism among others. Bones also communicate with other organs and tissues in the body. For humans, one way of naturally maintaining levels of this hormone in the blood, especially as we age, is exercise. In our evolutionary past this is likely to have been a survival hormone to escape predators and remember where to find food.*

**David Cox:** Does the key to anti-ageing lie in the bones?
*Observer 04/07/2020*

# Feet

*There is nothing more human than a human footprint.*

**Ai Wei Wei** (international Chinese artist)

\*\*\*

Hands and feet convey complex messages to and from our brains about our interactions with the world around us. The feet, in particular, give us feedback about the surfaces we walk on and the relationship of the feet to the rest of the body. If we are gripping the ground with our toes, or our weight is more in the heels, this may reflect compensatory patterns elsewhere in the body. Such observations are fundamental to Alexander.

The soles of our feet are extremely sensitive; there is a rich network of over 200,000 nerve endings in each sole, including the tips of the toes, which sends information to the brain about the ground beneath them. (Elephants 'listen' through the soles of their feet to vibrations travelling through the ground, coming from the feet of other elephants).

The reason we don't feel the full weight of our bodies on our feet, as they make contact with the ground, is because this pressure stimulates a reflex response in our postural muscles deep in our legs and near our spines. This reflex gives us a feeling of buoyancy as we walk, 'a spring in our step.'

The thought of our legs dangling like pendulums from our lower torsos rather than from our hip joints facilitates the action of the big, diagonal psoas muscles which stretch from the low back area through the pelvis to the inside of the upper thighs. This free movement in the legs helps the ankles to release, which in turn allows our feet to flex more easily as we move (unless we wear shoes which stop the feet bending !). It is useful to regularly circle the wrists and ankles, to keep these complex joints moving freely.

It was partly the unique structure of the human foot that gave us the speed to survive as hunters. Leonardo da Vinci considered the human foot, with its fantastic weight suspension system, to be a masterpiece of engineering and a work of art. The human foot is a strong and complex mechanical structure containing a quarter of all bones in the human body: 26 bones, plus 12 tendons and 18 muscles, stretching and flexing. As with any arch, the main arch in the foot gets stronger under stress — a highly tensile web: the harder you push down, the tighter its parts mesh and the Achilles tendon stores and releases energy. *The dome shape of this arch is echoed in the pelvic floor, the diaphragm, roof of the mouth, top of the orbits and skull.*

\*\*\*

Human beings and their ancestors have walked upright for over three million years; it is bipedalism that has made us human. Our ancestors walked or ran, mostly barefoot, or with minimal foot covering, on natural surfaces and, in some parts of the world, this is still the case. Barefoot running requires landing on the ball of the foot not the heel, whereas we naturally land on the heel when walking. It is no accident that marathon runners tend to come from nations where the barefoot state is still common from infancy to adulthood.

*The beautiful thing about running barefoot or in minimal footwear is that you are working with the body's natural proprioception, the ability to sense your own position in space. With nothing between you and the ground you get immediate sensory feedback with every step which encourages you to stay light on your feet and run with proper form.*

**Christopher McDougall**: *Born to Run.* 2009

\*\*\*

On the Welsh shore of the Severn estuary, archaeologists working on the Goldcliff excavations have revealed an eight-thousand-year-old fossil salt marsh so well preserved that human footprints look recent.

> *Some of the prints, left in loose mud are big and sloshy; others clean and crisp. You can see the pads of the toes and the mud that welled up between them: in some places the people had slipped and skidded, the tracks show how their heels swung round, their toes splayed to retain their balance... I looked again at these footprints receding across the marsh and into time...* ***and I felt I knew better who I was: where I have come from; what I still am.***

**George Monbiot**: *Feral — Rewilding the Land, Sea and Human Life*. 2014

✳✳✳

In 2007 I went to Kunming, a city in Yunnan, south-west China where my son was living. One day we were walking behind an old lady and my son said, '*look mum, bound feet*'. The woman heard us and clearly understood what he had said, because she turned round and looked right up at us — she was tiny and we are both tall (seen as very tall in China) — and an extraordinarily expressive smile lit up her whole face. It was as if her history of undoubted suffering was being witnessed; it is now very rare to see bound feet in China. The factory in Shanghai which made their special 'lotus shoes' closed in 2009.

This most brutal practice of distorting and binding small children's feet started about ten thousand years ago and lasted well into the 20th century. By 1949, when Mao took power, it remained in only a few remote areas.

If for no other reason than to honour those millions of women who suffered such torture, we must cherish our own feet and have gratitude for their unfettered condition, both men and women.

# Chapter 6
# Body Memory

## Icebergs of Biography

*It took a few seconds for my life to fall together, icebergs of biography looming through the fog: who I was, where I was, what I was doing, what I was doing there, who was waking me.*

**William Gibson**: *Hinterlands*, from Burning Chrome. 1986

\*\*\*

As I write, I have a photograph of snowdrops in the snow on my desktop. I can smell the snow and hear the crunch of footsteps. I can breathe in the cool freshness of the snowdrops. Is this body memory?

During an Alexander session, when we touch someone, we touch their lives and their stories about themselves. When teachers use hands-on work with students, it is likely to be a complex and multi-layered interaction, with both people carrying their unique colouring of body memory.

We store the whole physical and emotional history of our lives in our bodily tissues, in our nervous systems, in our brains, in our whole-body landscape. Our bodies and minds echo with the history of our ancestors, plus the imprint and the images of our culture. Our subjective memory of our own history is likely to be an important aspect of how we define ourselves. This core material, which we all carry as adults, shapes the styles, habits, behaviour, perceptions and attitudes that help to define us as individuals. Much of this process may exert its influence subconsciously, but it colours our responses to the major themes of life and our choice of allegiances.

For reasons of survival, we tend to retain traumatic memories in our bodies more than joys. I once heard this described as 'footprints on our souls.'

For more information on this topic, see chapter on 'Sweet Science', **Deane Juhan**: *Job's Body*. Barrytown/Station Hill Press, 3rd edition 2003.

\*\*\*

## Embodied Memory

*Every time I step*
*from the medium of this dry breath*
*from land to water*
*I am re-clothed*
*in the movement of liquid on my skin.*
*My spine elongates,*
*extends the breath*
*to outstretched limbs,*
*fingers, toes,*
*awakens embodied memory.*
*And as I swim*
*my breathing, amplified,*
*excites ancient molecules of breath*
*exhaled*
*by remote human ancestors*
*who once watched*
*shadows changing over the sea*
*or sat by firelight*
*and listened*
*to the breathing of the waves.*

**Genny (Gentian) Rahtz**: Embodied Memory, from *Sky Burial*. 2010

# Mirror Neurons

The book 'Awakenings' is an extraordinary and moving account of what happened when survivors of the 1920's sleeping sickness epidemic were given L-dopa, a drug for Parkinson's. The patient quoted below, whether talking about others or of music, is speaking of 'the mysterious touch', the contact of two existences. She is evoking what might be called the sense of communion, and she is likely to be describing the action of 'mirror neurons.'

> *When you walk with me I feel within me your own power of walking. I partake of the power and freedom you have... I partake of other people as I partake of music...*

**Oliver Sacks**: *Awakenings* — epilogue. 1973

\*\*\*

I once had an uncanny experience of something of the above when I volunteered to work with a mime street artist in York. I found I could effortlessly 'echo' his dance movements with my own body so long as I held his gaze. No doubt mirror neurons were involved. I believe this process of transmission can happen in master classes for professional performers of any kind, and also in Alexander sessions.

We learn by both imitating and watching. A mirror neuron is a specialist motor neuron that fires both when an animal acts, and when an animal observes the same action performed by another. Thus, the neuron 'mirrors' the behaviour of the other. Fascinating studies illustrate this process in many infant-parent interactions. Mirror neurons are a relatively recent discovery in neuroscience, with wide implications for medicine, education and performing artists of every kind... and clearly, for Alexander.

Mirror neurons have been directly observed in both human and primate species and also in birds. They form part of the capacity to understand others and empathise with them. Our need for each other is so critical to our survival that mechanisms in our body have been recruited to ensure we seek out relationships and strive to maintain them. We are familiar with how people often match gesture, voice tone and vocabulary — but this may also extend to their heart rate, blood pressure, body temperature, levels of circulating neurochemistry and brain activation patterns. As yet, we do not fully understand what triggers this phenomenon, but the fact that we see it in healthy interactions, and particularly where a close bond is present, suggests that it is fundamental to the ties that bind us, is likely to involve mirror neurons, and is key to the health benefits of social behaviour.

*** 

A mixture of remembering our own experience of an activity and resonating with a performance, live or on film, for example, is a very important function of the performing arts, and of sport; we go along for the neurological and chemical ride... We quite literally sense some sort of echo/activation in our own bodies as we follow movement in a live performer or in a film. Even if I just read books about climbing or surfing, I am subtly aware of their effect on my own neuro-musculature.

Alexander work increases our conscious awareness of how we might use the least amount of muscular effort appropriate to an activity. When we watch a sporting performance, we are appreciating the ability to generate the *precise amount of effort required...* the art that conceals art, and in doing so, looks effortless. This equally applies to top footballers and top dancers...

I wonder what Alexander himself would have thought of 'grime artists,' many of whom can coordinate voice, movement and music with an exquisite degree of artistic judgement.

Dance raises the coordination of muscular activity to an extreme. In classical ballet, we admire the dancer's ability to overcome his or her individual idiosyncrasies in order to reproduce painstakingly standardised purities of form. But in contemporary dance we may sometimes admire something very different: the inventiveness and spontaneity of the dancer, the ability to embody an intensely personal vision.

\*\*\*

*Her performance reminded me of why I first fell in love with ballet. Nothing she did was technically extraordinary, nothing was showy, her legs hardly ever rose above the horizontal. But such was her transparency, so profound was her identification with the role, that you couldn't really see the dancing. All was character, all was emotion, all was story. Glurjidze stopped time, and that is what great dancing can do.*

**Luke Jennings**: dance critic. *Observer* 19.1.2019
Elena Glurjidze is a senior principal ballerina from Georgia.

# Fascia

## the largest sense organ in the body

Jackie Chan and Bruce Lee, famous martial artists in the 1970s and '80s developed the ability to make their fascia ripple as they moved, which could be seen on the surface of their bodies, like a ripple building into a wave at sea. We can experience some sense of the fascia by splaying out our hands and holding them in a strong backwards stretch, then very slowly, letting them go, to feel the elastic recoil.

*** 

Our personal history shapes our fascia. It shrinks to accommodate our habitual range of movement, which contributes towards creating recognisable body silhouettes and characteristic ways of moving, as we grow older. A child's freedom of movement expresses the elastic quality of their fascia. Accordingly, an appreciation of this component of our connective tissue is fundamental to Alexander practice.

Fascia forms a latticework of fibrous tissue, a continuous layer under the skin and throughout the body, in places more like cling-film, and made mainly of collagen. Every nerve, muscle bundle, muscle fibre, blood vessel, organ, bone, tendon and ligament is enclosed in fascia, and there is fluid in between and within the fascial sheets to reduce friction. Fascia enables the body to work as one unit in coordinated patterns of movement and is one of the primary organising elements of our bodies. It differs widely in character and function throughout the body while both protecting and supporting the skeleton.

Until recently, the study of fascia, like that of kinaesthesia, was rather neglected by Western medicine but is now attracting more attention; surgeons are likely to follow its compartments and planes for keyhole surgery. Recent discoveries reveal that fascia is *the largest sense organ in the body*, the most richly innervated tissue with a very high density of sensory receptors.

The subtle energy channels or meridians utilised by Eastern medicine practitioners, such as acupuncturists, are thought to lie between the fascial layers.

Fascia becomes more fluid when it is activated but can also harden and de-hydrate, becoming inflamed and thickened. Animals keep their fascia healthy with a wide range of frequent stretches and movement. Research on the thickening of fibrotic processes involved in decreased mobility, where the layers of fascia and muscle do not glide so easily, suggests this may be helped by sustained slow stretching. If done slowly and calmly with an awareness of bodily sensations and breathing, it has better results, as in yoga. Joints need to be put through their full range of movement fairly regularly otherwise this range may gradually reduce. Stretching also counteracts the effects of a sedentary lifestyle and moves the blood, lymph, cerebro-spinal fluid and subtle energy, 'qi' or 'chi'.

Chinese medicine recognises that stagnant subtle energy can be a cause of pain, hence the alleviation of many aches and pains by slow, mindful stretching.

## Fascial Stretches

Alexander practice is particularly focussed on making a sensitive contact between muscle and mind and getting them to work together. But for many students this cannot easily happen until their muscle tone is reduced. As the adrenaline subsides, their nervous systems become calmer.

Teachers may initially make a quiet contact with 'non-doing' hands, making sure that they are not stimulating any muscular response, such as the 'startle pattern' (a fear response which tightens the body) or the flexor muscles' withdrawal reflex.

At some stage during an Alexander session, it often becomes apparent that there is constriction in the connective tissue, especially in the fascial framework, which is likely to be long-standing adaptive shortening. The fascia that encloses the muscle needs stretching and the potential range of movement of each muscle may also need increasing.

\*\*\*

# Fascial Stretch Procedures

*I have included this section for the Alexander Community as this aspect of the work can be neglected. It is towards the therapeutic rather than re-educational end of the Alexander spectrum.*

Fascial stretches can identify and target specifically compressed areas that otherwise remain a problem and can also improve body alignment. Unless the fascia is responsive, a student cannot easily experience how one part of their body influences other parts. A useful analogy is that of pulling one corner of a tablecloth to observe how it affects the whole cloth.

Fascial stretches can be applied to the spine, including neck and sacrum, and to the limbs. Decompression of the spine, while a student is lying on the table, is a slow, careful process which feels wonderfully calming. It requires an Alexander teacher to 'stay back' with their attention while holding the student's neck and 'listening' into the spine, sensing the degree of elasticity of each section. This helps the student to locate tighter areas of their spine; as they soften in these areas the teacher can then gradually take up the slack.

This stretch on the fascia must be slow and sensitive enough to allow a continual release of muscle, as well as stretching the fascia. A more physical, mechanical stretch could elicit muscular contraction which would be counter-productive! When we do slow mindful stretches ourselves this does not usually activate a reflex muscular contraction.

Once the fascia has been opened up the muscles can come to their full resting length. A student will then be able to breathe more freely and be open, mentally and physically, to taking this extra freedom of movement into any activity.

# Chapter 7
# Coming to Rest

## Constructive Rest and Meditation

*This sperm whale is resting vertically in the sea with half its brain asleep.*
© Paul Hilton and Greenpeace

\*\*\*

*Coming to Rest* has a clear relationship to *Inhibition* but is more about valuing or prioritising the fundamentally therapeutic process of taking a longer period of time for the nervous system, the mind, body and spirit to re-balance and settle into a quiet state. This facilitates the skill, central to Alexander, of regularly giving time for the system to 'come out of gear', to come to rest, *which reduces the habitual patterns of one activity colouring those following.*

Many of us have forgotten, or are unable to meet, one of our most basic needs which is to rest, to balance *doing* with simply *being.* Alexander can facilitate our ability to re-find this balance by helping us to connect body and mind, by being more self-aware, by helping us to be more calm, more present.

The prescribing of anti-depressant drugs makes up a huge part of the UK health budget; chronic stress and anxiety, eating disorders and the inability to sleep are endemic. The WHO says that depression is now the leading cause of illness and disability worldwide. Too few of us can drop easily into rest, either mentally or physically. For some people, chronic overdrive and stress become a prelude to illness.

(see section on *The Autonomic Nervous System*)

\*\*\*

## Constructive Rest or Semi-supine

A core tenet of Alexander is taking time each day to lie down in 'constructive rest' or 'semi-supine' for about fifteen or twenty minutes, which involves lying on our backs on the floor with knees and elbows bent, feet flat on the floor. Our hands may rest below the front ribs, on the solar plexus area, where we can feel the movement of our breath.

Many people need a few paperbacks to give firm support under the head, to stop it dropping back. This position allows the curves of the neck and lumbar spine to lengthen. The influence of gravity allows the spine, which has supported us vertically, to relax, and the inter-vertebral discs begin to reflate. People with low back or sacroiliac problems could also try resting their lower legs on a sofa or across a chair seat, with vertical upper legs, allowing the weight of the pelvis to drop down from the knees.

A complementary procedure, also used in yoga, involves moving the feet closer to the pelvis, then lifting the pelvis up high so that the spine can hang from the back of the shoulders. Each section of the spine can then be slowly rolled down and opened out, starting at the shoulders and finishing with the pelvis. This sequence further decompresses the spine and magically 'unlocks' the lumbar and sacral area as the spine releases.

*Both these procedures offer the chance to sink our attention into all the back areas of our bodies, perhaps visualising our imprint on warm sand. Our backs have sturdy layers of muscle which include the muscular anchors for all four limbs. This is in clear contrast to the very different, more receptive, expressive character of the front of our bodies. The space before us is also where we habitually give most of our attention.*

For many people, this position of rest feels like a psychological relief, a 'listening to the earth' underneath our backs, heads and feet. I use the phrase *taking refuge in our backs*, whether applied to lying in a horizontal position or when upright. Another useful phrase, *the weft and warp of the back*, the width and length stretching together, comes from the weaving industry.

One of the benefits of 'semi-supine' is that it can help us to become more aware of imbalances between the two sides of the body and hence the two hemispheres of the brain, each of which affects the functioning of the opposite side of the body, as with a stroke.

Taking time each day to come to stillness is a vital aspect of looking after ourselves, for breath, heart and mind to settle and to help us develop more awareness of our internal, felt sense, our kinaesthetic sense. We may keep our eyes shut to register the subtlety of these internal sensations. If they are open, we may notice those other senses which relate to our relationship with the world outside ourselves.

\*\*\*

*This very ancient remains of a tree trunk has 'come to rest' on a beach in Lincolnshire. It has an uncanny resemblance to the character of the human spine.*

## Stopped in our Tracks

We can be stopped in our tracks by a work of art in any medium, by a performance, a sporting event, a view, a new-born and also by seeing wild creatures in their natural environment — all our senses may be alert, and we are likely to feel awe or reverence... although this may be a remnant of the hunting instinct...

\*\*\*

## Meditation

*But my unlucky head that was always to let me know it was born to make my body miserable...*

**Daniel Defoe** (1660–1731): Robinson Crusoe.

\*\*\*

There is a wide range of meditation practices across the world but the basic principle of coming to stillness, to an awareness of the present moment, to 'recollecting' our sense of ourselves, is becoming more familiar in the West. This skill is particularly useful for both Alexander students and teachers as it requires a degree of mental alertness and expanded attention, coupled with relaxed muscles. It also offers the chance to re-balance our systems between the adrenaline fuelled sympathetic nervous system (fight or flight) and the calming, relaxing parasympathetic system (rest and renewal).

(see section on *The Autonomic Nervous System*)

* * *

Meditation can be a helpful aspect of Alexander practice.

> *There is no doubt I was in pieces when I started the training, both mentally and physically. I wanted to find a way back to myself and finding this connection was a core part of my experience during training. I needed grounding, landing back into my body, into my immediate surroundings, into the sensations of my breath. During the training, meditation helped me to find a relationship between my mind and my body. It gave me an opportunity to pay attention to my physical sensations, to all my senses and to gradually learn the skill of returning my attention to the present moment, to my posture and to the rhythm of my breathing.*

> **Judit Pasztor**: student at SEAS Alexander school, now a teacher.

* * *

It takes time to settle into a quiet meditative state, like a bird easing into its nest and re-arranging twigs or moss and grasses. We may wrap a shawl around ourselves and change our seating or our sitting position, perhaps light a candle.

It also takes time to notice patterns of physical tension and to allow mental or emotional 'froth' to come to the surface. This may gradually settle when we expand our attention into the space surrounding us. During this process, perhaps with some degree of humour, we may learn what it means for the mind to 'get out of the way', to take a back seat, to be just an 'observing mind', to be more at ease with the world around us! This becomes easier and can touch places of more depth with regular sitting practice. The breath can be like an anchor — returning our attention to the whole of the inbreath, the whole of the outbreath.

\*\*\*

Various forms of mindful, meditational movement such as qi gong, nei gong, tai chi, and yoga, or walking in silence in powerful landscapes, can be alternative routes to a meditational state, or as practices which precede sitting meditation.

> *I walk barefoot on warm clay*
> *and notice a sense of self*
> *requiring less ballast*
> *of thoughts or feelings*

\*\*\*

Eastern cultures have a long tradition of physical and mental disciplines for the development of the human spirit and for psychological and physical health, some of which are increasingly being embraced by Western cultures. But Alexander, in particular, is too little acknowledged as a Western version of such practices that link mindful movement with the breath and with conscious awareness, in a wide variety of contexts, or as part of spiritual practice.

*\*\*\**

There follows a verbatim example of one of Don Burton's more anatomically based meditation sessions at Fellside Alexander School, which may clarify its relevance for the Technique. He said that meditating was an '*act of ecological and spiritual sanity.*'

> *Be aware of the weight of the head, 5 kilos or more, and how the skull balances on the atlas. Think of the roof of the mouth releasing upwards as a continuation of the spine. If you listen, you can change the muscle tone of the whole body — listening and balance are closely connected. Relax the jaw muscles behind the ears and under the cheek bones. Take one step back in the mind, not in the forebrain but further back into the sensory part of the brain. Start by softening behind the eyes — this changes the facial expression and opens the face. (It closes when people put attention into the frontal area). Be present with physical sensations for each bit of the body. Don't visualise diagrams of the body. Drop anchor, take a back seat, find the breath, release armpits and collar bones, widen attention.*

> **Don Burton**

*\*\*\**

The photograph of the sleeping sperm whale at the beginning invites the following extract at the end.

> *With the landless gull, that at sunset folds her wings and is rocked to sleep between billows, so at nightfall, the Nantucketeer,\* out of sight of land, furls his sails and lays him to his rest, while under his very pillow rush herds of walruses and whales.*

**Herman Melville**: *Moby Dick.* 1993

\*\*\*

(Moby Dick was first published in the USA in 1851. Petroleum was first found in Pennsylvania in 1859, which gradually replaced the huge demand for whale oil).

---

\* a sailor from the sperm whale-fishing community in Nantucket, Mass. USA.

# The Autonomic Nervous System

Alexander helps us to notice how we might find a balance between 'doing' and 'being', how to re-charge our batteries with periods of rest and relaxation, to become more aware of whether we are in rhythm or out of step. It also helps us to recognise when and why we may be running on adrenaline.

The Autonomic Nervous System (ANS) is involuntary and has evolved for our survival so that we can respond to danger; its two branches regulate arousal throughout the body and work with the endocrine system.

The **sympathetic** branch, mobilising the body's resources, gets us ready for action — *fight, flight or freeze* — It involves adrenaline and the stress hormone, cortisol and is likely to shut down the processes of digestion.

The **parasympathetic** branch slows us down — *replenishment, repair and renewal* — which includes helping the processes of digestion, and is activated by rest and relaxation.

A focus on long, slow outbreaths will activate the parasympathetic aspect of the ANS and help panic or anxiety attacks. Conversely, if we breathe with short, hasty breaths which are likely to be mainly in the upper chest, we will activate the sympathetic system.

In Western society, our nervous systems are often working on the sympathetic nervous system for long periods of time. A 'non-doing', quiet Alexander hand contact can start to shift the body chemistry and activate the parasympathetic system. The semi-supine position of rest, and meditation, may do the same.

Stress generally produces a high level of autonomic arousal, although in the longer term it can elicit the opposite: a shutdown, lethargic, depleted state. When we are at our best, these two autonomic systems work closely together, affecting all the organs of the body, to keep us in an optimum state of engagement with our environment and with ourselves.

\*\*\*

The book below offers useful information on how we may learn to re-balance our ANS:

**David Servan-Schreiber:** *Healing without Freud or Prozac — natural approaches to curing stress, anxiety and depression.* Rodale International Ltd. 2004

# Chapter 8
# A Wider Context

## Breathing

### breathing in the natural world

The Latin word *spiritus* means breath, the origin of the word spirit. *Pneuma* is the ancient Greek word for breath which can also mean spirit or wind; like the wind, the breath is always changing.

\*\*\*

F M Alexander was called 'the breathing man' and he promoted himself as 'the founder of a respiratory method'. His own vocal and respiratory problems drove him to explore how his ingrained, habitual ways of using his body, which included his thoughts, could affect his breathing.

Central to Alexander is the process of discovering how, why and when we cramp or distort our breathing mechanisms. We learn to become more aware of what it means to *not interfere* with the natural ebb and flow of the breath. Everything we encounter, our thoughts, our feelings, our imagination, influences how we inhabit our bodies and the coherence of our breathing, as any vocalist or wind player will confirm.

The diaphragm, a big muscle that facilitates breathing, resembles an upturned ladle with the handle in the low back and the bowl under the lower ribs. This muscle is anchored into the low back and under the front ribs, so we may feel the swelling of the inbreath in our bellies, the back of our low ribs, or as a widening in the waist area. But for many adults, tension in the neck, jaw, shoulders and spine all play havoc with this free movement of the breath. This may be compounded by a habit of restricting breathing to the chest and holding tension in the solar plexus, between navel and ribs.

Keeping the nape of the neck spacious influences the crucial role of the phrenic nerve, with its roots in the vertebrae of the neck. This nerve helps to control the diaphragm. It can be remembered using the mnemonic: 'c 3, 4 and 5 keeps the diaphragm alive' (c — the cervical part of the spine — neck).

If we watch a young child sleeping, we can see that their entire body is naturally in rhythmic motion, expanding and softening as they breathe. During an Alexander session, adults may also experience 'being breathed', as if the entire body is breathing of its own accord; it can feel visceral and yet ethereal at the same time. The ability to breathe is one of the more fundamental characteristics of being alive.

\*\*\*

Reading the following passage from a work of fiction, 'The Hunter', is likely to elicit an awareness of our whole breathing mechanism.

> *Darkness falls; the stars take their infinite curtain call. He sits and feels his body grow light, disappear, so now there is no skin between himself and the plateau. He expands. The huge deep ground he is sitting on is holding him up: he is nowhere, everywhere. When he breathes he can sense the air cool as it flows over the moisture in his nostrils, his belly swells, then the same air, a little warmer, flows out again. This is what he focuses on: the air in, the air out and in time there is nothing but something through which air passes, just as it passes through the shivering treetops below him, over stones, slips through blades of grass. The black night grows cold and still he sits.*

> **Julia Leigh**: *The Hunter*. 2000
> (a novel set in Tasmania where F M Alexander grew up)

***

## Trees

Trees are the lungs of our planet. They take in carbon dioxide from the air, use sunlight as energy to turn that carbon dioxide into sugars, and then use those sugars as their food. By this process, trees and other plants make oxygen. (Phytoplankton in the seas also take in carbon dioxide and produce more than half of the oxygen on the planet).

The chemistry of our breathing involves the opposite process. We inhale oxygen, nitrogen, argon and water vapour and exhale carbon dioxide, one of the principal waste products of metabolism. We can last for considerably longer without breathing in oxygen than we can tolerate the build-up of carbon dioxide, so a long, slow outbreath can be very restorative.

The shape of our lungs resemble upside down trees with the windpipe resembling a tree trunk and the alveoli, or air sacs, being like twigs.

\*\*\*

We may recognise, and feel in our own bodies, how the rhythms of our own breath find echoes in the cycles of nature on land. People who live in more temperate climates may notice the almost imperceptible breath of sap rising in plants and trees in spring, and its slow return to earth in autumn.

\*\*\*

Many of us have also experienced sitting on a beach, becoming aware of synchronising our breathing with the waves. Breathing is one of the few bodily functions over which we can have conscious control but which can also be involuntary, or automatic.

\*\*\*

## Estuaries

The semidiurnal incoming sea tides are like an inbreath, drawn up the riverbeds of estuaries, as salt water is heavier than fresh water. The river water flows out above the salt water, like an outbreath, out to sea.

\*\*\*

## Migrations of Animals

*The movement of animals in the Arctic is especially compelling because the events are compressed into a few short months. Migratory animals like the bowhead whale and the snow goose often arrive on the last breath of winter... They come north in staggering numbers... Standing there on the ground, you can feel the land filling up, feel something physical in it under the influence of the light, an embrace or exultation. Watching the animals come and go and feeling the land swell up to meet them and then feeling it grow still at their departure, I came to think of these migrations as a breath, as the land breathing. In spring a great inhalation of light and animals. The long-bated breath of summer. And an exhalation that propelled them all south in the fall.*

**Barry Lopez**: *Arctic Dreams*. 2014

# Unity with the Natural World

F M Alexander emphasised the essential unity of mind and body. Psycho-spiritual unity could be understood as part of this picture, and must include our unity with the natural world. Inevitably, Alexander was 'of his time'. He perceived the human ability to be self-aware, and able to control responses to stimuli in a rational and conscious manner, as an indication that human evolution was propelling humans to rise above 'primitive' animal instincts.

Times have now changed in a very fundamental way; we are re-learning that humans are an integral part of the natural world, not apart from it, as indigenous people have always known. Many people in the Alexander community and others will know how their relationship with the natural environment has an influence on how they work on themselves, or with other people. In the section on *Expanded Attention* I describe an Alexander session with Don Burton which included working with our experience of the landscape. When I was with Alexander groups in Greece, we felt that our work was imbued with the presence of the local old olive trees, that we shared the same ground.

It is no wonder that we neglect the natural world outside ourselves when, generally speaking, many of us neither know much about the insides of our own bodies nor how they function, nor take much notice of our sense of being embodied, our kinaesthetic sense.

Most human beings now live in cities and it could be said that we are evolving into city animals. It has been estimated that four out of five European citizens are living in urban areas, which, to some extent, insulate us against the forces of nature. It has taken the growing ecological crisis to remind us of the essential fragility of this insulation.

We do know, literally deep in our bones, that we are part of the mammalian animal world whose skeletons are, in many respects, similar to our own. Most have seven cervical (neck) vertebrae, although they differ in the total number of vertebrae and in the relative proportions of their bones. The design of our human skeleton echoes through that of, say, an ape, cat, dog, horse, mouse or sheep. Even whales' skeletons are recognisably related to our own, although missing pelvis and legs.

\*\*\*

The British scientist and inventor James Lovelock has spent many years researching his hypothesis, now called *Gaia Earth Systems Science*, that all life on earth is a self-regulating community of organisms interacting with each other and with their surroundings.

This hypothesis reverberates with Alexander's idea that our bodies have an essential intelligence, an *original order*, an innate drive to health and equilibrium, long recognised by holistic therapists. He emphasised learning what it means to *not interfere* with this delicate mechanism, to *get out of the way of natural good use of ourselves.* Isabella Tree's book, 'Wilding', quoted at the end, describes the far-reaching results of allowing natural processes to restore farm land to its more natural state.

\*\*\*

Nature is about change. It can teach us so much about time and rhythm, growth and decay, about waking up to our senses. Whether we notice these influences or not, we are radically affected by what grows around us, by the landscape, the light, the weather and the cycles of nature, although we, in turn, radically affect our natural environment.

We are also influenced by the immense bodies of seawater that speak to the water inside us. When we are young our bodies are, on average, about 60% water, a percentage that reduces with age. Our bodies are made of the same minerals as the Earth.

I once spent a night in a tent above the high tide line on a pebble beach on the south coast. In the night, as the tide came in, I could hear the sea getting louder and was aware of its influence on the fluid in my body — it was a feeling of being in communion with the sea, as if my whole body was listening to its motion.

\*\*\*

*The need to relate to the landscape and to other forms of life —
whether one considers this urge aesthetic, emotional, cognitive or
even spiritual — is in our genes. Sever that connection and we are
floating in a world where our deepest sense of ourselves is lost...*

*A pleasure that comes from being surrounded by living organisms
is rooted in our evolution. We have been hunter-gatherers for 99%
of our genetic history, totally and intimately involved with the
natural world...*

*Our responses to nature, in particular the ability to be calmed
and reassured by natural settings and views, are located in a
much older, deeper part of our brain, the limbic system, that
generates our survival reflexes.*

**Isabella Tree**: *Wilding.* 2018

# References

My material from Don Burton comes from a variety of sources — from Alexander Teachers Network newsletters, some videos of Don, and my own notes, made over three years at Fellside Alexander School, plus discussions and other students' notes.

Alexander, F M: *The Use of the Self*. Methuen 1985 (first published 1932).

Bloch, Michael: *The Life of F M Alexander*. Little, Brown 2004.

Caldwell, Tommy: *The Push — a climber's journey of endurance, risk and going beyond limits*. Michael Joseph 2017. Also YouTube — *The Dawn Wall*.

Claxton, Guy: *Intelligence in the Flesh — why your mind needs your body much more than it thinks*. YUP 2016.

Defoe, Daniel: *Robinson Crusoe* (first published 1719).

Finnegan, William: *Barbarian Days — a surfing life*. Little Brown 2015.

Frankl, Victor E: *Man's Search for Meaning*. 1946 (in German). Rider 2004.

Gibson, William: *Count Zero*. Gollancz 1986.

Gibson, William: *Burning Chrome*. Gollancz 1986.

Grandin, Temple: *The Autistic Brain*. Rider 2014.

Grunwald, Peter: *Eye Body: the art of integrating eye, brain and body*. Condevis 2008.

Juhan, Deane: *Job's Body — A Handbook for Bodywork*. Barrytown/Station Hill Press Inc. 3$^{rd}$ edition 2003.

Leigh, Julia: *The Hunter*. Penguin 1990.

Lent, Jeremy: *The Patterning Instinct*. Prometheus books 2017.

Lieberman, Daniel: *The Story of the Human Body*. Penguin 2013.

Linn Geurts, Kathryn: *Culture and the Senses — bodily ways of knowing in an African community*. UCP 2002 (extract from synopsis on the web).

Lopez, Barry: *Arctic Dreams*. Vintage 2014.

Lovelock, James: *Gaia — a new look at life on earth*. OUP 2016.

McDougall, Christopher: *Born to Run*. Profile Books Ltd 2009.

McGilchrist, Iain: *The Master and his Emissary — the divided brain and the making of the Western world*. YUP 2010.

Melville, Herman: *Moby Dick*. Wordsworth Editions Ltd. 1993 (first published 1851).

Mitchell, Damo: *A Comprehensive Guide to Daoist Nei Gong*. Singing Dragon 2018.

Monbiot, George: *Feral — rewilding the land, sea and human Life*. Penguin 2014.

Pessoa, Fernando: *Poems of Fernando Pessoa*. City Lights Books 1998.

Rahtz, Genny (Gentian): *Sky Burial*. Flux Gallery Press 2010.

Rahtz, Gentian: *An Appreciation of the Visionary Contribution*

*Don    Burton Made to the Alexander Technique Community.* StatNews, vol. 9, no. 10, May 2018.

Sacks, Oliver: *Awakenings.* Picador 1973.

Servan-Schreiber, David: *Healing without Freud or Prozac — natural approaches to curing stress, anxiety and depression.* Rodale International Ltd. 2004.

Tree, Isabella: *Wilding.* Picador 2018.

White, Jonathan: *Tides — the science and spirit of the ocean.* Trinity University Press 2017.

# Permissions

The author is grateful to the following individuals and publishers for permission to reproduce their material.

John Hunter — including quotations from his blog on John Hunter's web page — www.upward-thought.com.

-----------------

Aleksandra.

Judit Pasztor.

Miranda Tufnell.

-----------------

Philip Cross — tree trunk photograph.

Paul Hilton and Greenpeace — sperm whale photograph.

William Rahtz — children's photographs.

-----------------

## Little, Brown Book Group Ltd.

William Finnegan: *Barbarian Days — a surfing life*. Corsair 1998.

-----------------

## Pan Macmillan

Isabella Tree: *Wilding*. Picador 2018.

-----------------

## The Permissions Company LLC

Fernando Pessoa: *Poems. The Keeper of Sheep*. City Lights Books, San Francisco 1998.

------------------

## Random House Group Ltd — Penguin Books.

Tommy Caldwell: *The Push*. Michael Joseph 2017.

George Monbiot: *Feral*. Allen Lane 2013.

Barry Lopez: *Arctic Dreams*. Vintage 1986.

**Gentian Rahtz** BA Hons, M Ed, STAT (Cert)

At Hull University I was involved with the thriving poetry and arts scene, supported by the Chief Librarian, Philip Larkin, and I became one of the Hull poets. I completed an M Ed in Art Education in 1981 at Manchester University and worked for the Open University for twelve years, teaching a ground-breaking, multi-media course in basic creative processes called 'Art and Environment'. A collection of my poems, 'Sky Burial', was published by The Flux Gallery Press in 2010.

I qualified as an Alexander Technique teacher in 1990, from the three-year training course at Fellside School in Kendal, UK, directed by Don Burton, and later, also trained as a craniosacral therapist. I have taught Alexander in a variety of contexts, including York University music department, for over thirty years, and also attempt to play the shakuhachi, a Japanese bamboo flute.

My son, who works as an interpreter, has taken some of the photographs for 'Seeing with Fresh Eyes.'

**http://gentian-alexander-oxford.co.uk**

Lightning Source UK Ltd.
Milton Keynes UK
UKHW020919251122
412773UK00018B/1198

9 781399 914062